The 10 Must-Haves Qualities Men Look For In Women

What Men Don't Want You To Know

By: Stephen Jones

Introduction

I want to thank you and congratulate you for downloading the book, *"The 10 Must-Haves Qualities Men Look For In Women: What Men Don't Want You To Know"*.

This book contains proven steps and strategies on how to become the woman everyman would desire. I have outline 10 must-haves quality every woman most have, given you some reasons why men would never what you to know that they are really in search of these characters, and funny enough not many people realize this. Although they are quite aware that there are some qualities that they need to have in other to make a man trip. But I am sure that you may not be aware that there are actually some charters that are compulsory to have as a woman.

Therefore, I would gladly advice that you study some of the different characters that I have outlined, have them at the back of your palm and ensure to develop any one that you do not have. You should also keep in mind that it might not be very easy to develop one, so you would have to persevere and keep pushing on. Your characters are what make you a real woman. Therefore, you would really want to consider having the best characters that would elevate your life and not take you down. That is why I took my time to outline these 10 different character that a couple of friends, colleagues, family and I have come to agree that every woman needs to consider and develop. Being a woman is never easy but when you have a bearing as to what you want and how to achieve it, it makes life a lot easier.

Thanks again for downloading this book, I hope you enjoy it!

The information herein is offered for informational purposes solely, and is universal as so. The presentation of the information is without contract or any type of guarantee assurance.

The trademarks that are used are without any consent, and the publication of the trademark is without permission or backing by the trademark owner. All trademarks and brands within this book are for clarifying purposes only and are the owned by the owners themselves, not affiliated with this document.

Chapter 1

Being a woman in this modern world that we live in now is not as easy as it use to be. I am sure that many women out there would agree with me. These days a lot is being expected from a woman, and very little attention is given to them on how to achieve them. In addition, with the fast-growing rate of civilization, everything just seems to get even more complicated. With a whole lot of "DOs" and "DON'Ts," what is right from wrong may look far from being clear. Sometimes as a woman, you may just need a break from everything, and you know just thieve and live your life like you are the only one on earth.

In the midst of thieving and living your life without giving any regards to what anyone feels or think, perhaps just at that moment, you notice this particular guy that made you feel butterflies in your Tommy, and you are wondering what is happening to you. Without asking for much of your consent, you notice you are already genuinely in love with this person, and you are like oh no! Your mind is racing as you are wondering if this a good thing or a bad thing? Then, you are asking yourself what to do next?

Peradventure you conclude that you are in love with this guy like you are head over heels in love with him, and all you can think about is how to be just by his side, to hold him, and all that not people do when they are in love. Then you ask yourself the big question, how do I make this person attracted to me? What should I do to make him fall in love with me? Are there some hidden qualities that if I should possess this person would be utterly and entirely in love with me? Some may question just start rumbling into your head.

Now what I am going to give to you is more like a strategy that would help you improve yourself and at the end if you can be diligent enough with the approach. Then you can be sure that any man would be attracted to you, even that poor guy that doesn't know what is about to hit him would not be able to him himself but feel attracted to you. In this book, I am going to be highlighting 10 must have qualities men look for in women, and funny enough men do not really want you as a woman to know about these things. Therefore, I am going to be starting my list from the top to the least, so fasten your seatbelts as I take you down this road on an adventure to discovering who you really are in other to better improve yourself and your love life as a woman.

1. Family Oriented

Now first on my list of must-have qualities men look out for in women is being family oriented. Unbelievably but men who are quite severe for a long-term relationship would want to have a woman by their side who is family oriented. Many people have said many things about what is and what is not, but if a woman is not close to her own family, it sends a kind of aura to people around her that she is not family oriented. It may even get as bad as some people thinking that you may end up being a bad mom or you would make an exceptional homemaker or a home keeper.

Whatever the case may be, you need to ensure you are family oriented if you really what that guy to be attracted to you, or you just want to be attractive generally, then you need to really work on this quality. Moreover, if you recall a wise saying that says that charity begins at home, and what is charity, charity means merely love. Therefore, if you were not family oriented, if you are not in close contact and communication with your own family, you would find it so hard to show love. Perhaps you may feel infatuation and lust, but it would not be real genuine love.

Chapter 2

2. Insert **Kind-hearted**

Men also look for the quality of kindness in a woman. This actually attracts many men to a woman. You may just think or feel that there is not much to say or think about kindness, but the smallest gesture of service from a woman can win the heart of a man completely. Many times men would not allow you to know that they really value this character in a woman, probably because they feel shy about it. Man can be a bit secretive about what they want to see in a woman. It may be because they think that if they reveal what they want, probably a woman who is just after her own selfish interest may just fake these characters in other to attract the heart of the man.

As a woman and you do not have a kind heart, you should really work on it. Developing a kind heart may not really be so easy especially if you are a kind of person that looks after your own self, and do not really give too much attention to others. As a woman, it is not really so cute not to have a kind heart, because it can really cause many issues in the future especially when you start to bear children. Taking care of children can be a bit overwhelming, as you would need a kind heart in other to be able to take care of them.

Also, men love women that can actually make good care of their children.
To develop a kind heart, you need to start from the little-little gestures, like giving a smile to someone, or holding the door for someone to pass. Then from there, you can advance to a higher way of showing love like gifting may be a cloth to the poor, or food, you can even go as far as giving the poor money. These little gestures with time would take root in you, and you would realize that you are doing it without even putting much effort to it. You would find out that you are just kind by nature and not because you feel, you need to be kind.

Apart from the fact that when you are kind-hearted, it attracts men, because men seek this character in a woman. You would also notice that you would be more at peace with yourself. As you would even feel free. Your mind would give you a kind of feeling that makes you walk with boldness and confidence, as you know that no matter what anyone does to you, you are going to repay them with kindness, not willingly but unconsciously as consideration has become your nature.

I really do not know how else to explain it, perhaps just by the name kind-hearted would be just enough to do the job for you. Also, as a woman, you need to be thoughtful, as well as loving and caring. As you do those little things without putting so much thought as you why you do them is also a way of showing that you are a kindhearted woman. Also, as you smile as a woman towards someone and the person cannot help but smile back also shows that you radiate love from yourself. So whatever the case may be always strive to be kind-hearted in all your doings, do not repay evil with evil, because you never can tell who is just watching you just to see your reaction, maybe you would latch out, or you would just smile at any evil being done to you.

3. Intellectually Challenging

As a woman trying to be intellectually challenging at times. Most men just love this character in a woman, even though they might never say it to your face that you need to be a bit more challenging intellectually or to commend you that you are intellectually challenging, but rather men would just keep being men and let their pride cloud their good judgment. There is absolutely no need to deny the fact that as a woman, one thing or the other is what attracts a man to us. In other words, men seek some specific things in a woman. Also, when they find it, well, whatever happens, happens. However, you can be sure that love is bound to spring up in most cases.

Therefore, as a woman, you need to examine yourself from time to time, and one thing you also need to be on the lookout for is to be intellectually challenging. Being intellectually challenging goes far beyond what meets the eyes. When you are intellectually challenging, as woman men tend to generally find you more interesting, as you would find it so easy to keep up with any conversation.

What good is a relationship between a man and a woman if there is no proper communication? Now since an intellectually challenging woman can be conversations, then she would be able to connect with the man properly, and from connection to a relationship, and the list goes on and on as far as you may want it to be.

If as a woman you are not a conservationist or just a simple woman that is intellectually challenging, then you are going actually to be missing a whole lot of things. It is very encouraging to be intellectually challenging as it helps you to be able to understand and reason objectively on general and educational matters.

If you are intellectually challenging as a woman when your mind sights a problem, your first line of defense is to offer a solution to the problem, and this is what actually attracts men to this character. It helps everyone to become that true helpmate that they are meant to be. However, you see men will always be men, as they would not tell a woman that they need them to be helpful because they are men and men love that feeling of being in control. Men love always to be the one with the solution, they do not like being helped, or instead told what to do in the way of helping.

However, when a woman is intellectually challenging, she would help the man without her even realizing what she is doing. Since it is her nature, either by birth or something she just developed, the bottom line is that she would be more helpful this way.

Even your adrenaline rush tends to increase in a way especially when your intellects is processing a problem for a solution.

That thrilling moment can be a source of connection between the man and the woman, as men generally secrete more adrenaline than women do. As the adrenaline, level builds up, so down the release of dopamine also. Dopamine is a hormone secreted in the brain that is responsible for happiness. Now as for your dopamine level increase, you tend to feel a whole lot happier than you use to for no reason, and this happiness and smile all over your face makes you look a lot attractive as a woman. So, men look out for a woman with an intellectually challenging character a lot.

Chapter 3

4. An Understanding and Empathetic Woman

Next on my list is the character of being understanding and empathetic as a woman. This one of the most natural characters to develop is on this list. Moreover, it would not take anything for you nor cost you a dime to be more understanding and empathetic from time to time. I see no reason why any woman in this world should not understand. Men really hate a bragging wife or girlfriend, as it really does step on their nerves.

Understanding your partner is a huge step that you need to take in other to ensure that you and your partner can grow together. Understanding is an essential character every woman needs to have, as well as she needs to be empathetic. Men look for this feature above all know a woman, and funny enough, many women do not realize this. As a woman, you cannot go about doing things the way you want to. If you wish that your dream guy to come asking you out on a date, there are certain characters that you need to possess as a woman, and being understanding with an empathetic heart is one of them.

I wouldn't say that being understanding is going to be comfortable all the time, there would be times when you would just feel like letting all hell brake at times, especially when you are offended. However, despite this, you need to understand the fact that you are a woman, and the man is the head, so you need to give him that respect at first, and then try as much as you can to see reasons with him as to why he did whatever he did.

After understanding the reason why a person would do a particular thing to you, then you need also to have the heart that would be able to let go of it all. You cannot just understand and not forgive, forgiveness is vital, and it helps to ensure a stable relationship. Trying to understand someone actually means you are putting yourself in the person's shoes and try to see reasons with the person.

When you understand someone you actually participate attention to the person needs, perhaps you notice your partner needs a particular thing you just need to try your best to assist the partner. You do not really need to wait for your partner to ask for it before you offer it that is pure understanding. Men love this character in a woman so much, because men have pride as we know it, and they would not want to ask for something is even though they are in desperate need for it. Now if you as a woman posses these characters, then men would be attracted to you.

Also, when you really understand someone, you will even know when your partner needs your time. If you do not understand the times when you have to spend time with your partner, then you do not really have an understanding. Develop this character of intelligence and an empathetic heart so that you can be a better person, as well as help you are more attractive. Besides, after you develop these characters, you can say to yourself that you are on the right track to thriving in life.

5. Being Ambitious

For a woman to be ambitious can mean a whole lot of things, but one thing is sure that men love to see a woman being enthusiastic about her doings. To thrive a woman you need to know that having this character would help you achieve this also. Therefore, it is good for a woman to be ambitious, but not in a desperate way through. When a woman is determined, she just wants to improve her life.

Being ambitious as a woman means that you have dreams in your heart and you make arrangements and plans to achieve these dreams. Even though you know that the journey to achieving greatness is not a very smooth road, meaning that you know that you would encounter a lot of troubles and roadblock along the way. Despite all these challenges, you still desire to achieve your goals then you are definitely ambitious.

Being ambitious is not a very easy character to develop as a woman, as being a woman you tend to get pissed off by things easily. However, if only you can just persevere, the sky would not be your limit but your starting point, because as an ambitious woman your driving force is the depth of your vision you can see. Also, as far as your vision eyes can see that is what you are going to work on to achieve.

You may be wondering that why on earth would any man feel more into an ambitious woman, as they would kind of act as a kind of threat to the man regarding success. This is because many people believe that when a woman is more successful than a man is, it is more like the woman would become the man and the man would become the woman, as well as would the level of respect the woman has for the man would as well reduce drastically.

Now, even with this threat just hanging around the corner, peeping and waiting for the right time to come forth. Men still adore women that are ambitious. One main reason why men are into a determined woman is the sense of independence that an ambitious woman posses. Generally, no man would be so proud when his woman depends on him solely for everything that she needs. The truth is that even though he may feel all right with it initially, as time passes by he would lose interest and it would start to piss him off.

However, when you as a woman become ambitious about your dream. So just go out there, and you make waves, achieve greatness, invent a new technology just become more useful, and you would notice a significant turnaround in your love life. There is a famous street saying that says that forgets the girls, chase the money and the girls would case you. What this saying is just trying to portray to us is that no matter what may come I live do not get distracted by the pleasures of life, but stay focused in achieving greatness, and when you have finally realized that importance, the desires of like will come knocking at your door.

Now with the briefing I have given to you, I hope you are able to realize just how important being an ambitious woman is to attracting that man you have had in your mind for a very long time now. Therefore, instead of working on getting that man, I strongly urge you to work on yourself more extensively, and in the end, that man would be the one chasing you. The best part is that you would not only get the attention of the man and other men as well because no one sees a jewel and not appreciate it and want to have it, but you would also be working on yourself significantly.

Chapter 4

6. A consistent woman

To be a logical woman is more than just a character because this virtue can actually make any man fall for you instantly. When you are consistent in what you do, it means you do it continually with ease and pleasure. Take for example you love to cook, and you cook consistently any man that may not have noticed you before, would at least notice your food, and from there a conversation can be built on that and then a date and then whatever level you may wish to take the relationship to. However, the bottom line is consistency.

To be consistent in many areas of your life as a woman may not be so easy in this present world that we live in now. So many different things can derail you from your track of consistency. As long as you are consistent, I whatever situation you are doing there is bound to progress in your life. Apart from the fact that you would be able to master whatever it is you are consistent with, but it will also allow you to get through many tough times in life. Therefore, if you are consistent in anything you are doing, keep it up, as there is always a reward for diligent work.

You need to be consistent also to ensure that you can transform yourself, let us say you are trying to develop a new habit. If you are not consistent about it, let us tell you only practice occasionally or probably only when you feel the urge to exercise then there would be no significant changes in your life. To ensure full maximum effect you have to be consistent, even when you are feeling low, be consistent with it, or when you are tired still keep pushing on and at the end of the day, you would be surprised at the amount of progress that you would be able to make in so little time.

Still, on the issue of consistency, men love when they know their woman is consistent. If you take, for example, a man would feel more attracted to you as a woman if you consistently make him happy. Like you do it every time, maybe when he gets back from work, you walk up to him and pat him at his back, give him a warm hug, cheer him up, make his soul feel a lot lighter, then you would not even realize when he would just without control love you unconditionally. It takes just very few little things that you can put in mind as a woman that would make your man love you without condition, and being consistent with your dealings with him is one of them.

Now, let me explain to you in a layman term what consistency really is because men really look out for this character in women, and many women do not realize this. That is why you would see many women out there still single and unmarried, not because they choose not to get married, but because no one is asking for their hand in marriage. Marriage is a lifetime union, and no one would want to get into a lifetime union with the wrong person. That is why men are very particular about the things the lookout for in a woman because these things are what tells them if the woman is right, OK, or not up to what they want in a woman. If a woman is consistent in whatever she is doing, then she is most likely going to get a lot of attention from people.

7. Willingly to Put in Effort for your Sake

When a woman is willing to do things just for your sake can actually drive most men nuts. Because this is the highest form of love, you can feel for someone, when the person has control over your will now by force but because of the love that exists between the both of you.

You will want to cheer up your man is a typical example of what men look out for, or your will to want to keep that smile on his face. It is not necessarily, what you do that makes the heart of men pump with so much joy. However, the way that you do it drives them nut. The reason why you do it that actually really counts to them.

Let us talk another example or scenario, imagine your man is angry with you for a particular thing you did, maybe you are wearing a type of dress he disapproves of, and he is mad at you. You could make a deliberate and willing act of gesture towards his complaint and does something about your wardrobe, perhaps give off those clothes he disapproves of, and buy the best clothes that you feel he would really love to see you wearing.

Even though this whole process may seem a bit expensive to do just for the single purpose of telling the one you like that you are willing to please him. To be able to compel yourself to bid the will of others especially the one you love in place of your own will is not easy. Instead, it is just a sacrifice that you are willing to pay, a sacrifice of love.

If a woman knows that when she keeps on doing that special thing that attracts you without her even knowing exactly what she is doing. This is quite a great way for her to ensure that she can take advantage of making sure that you stay attracted to her at all time.

Even though it may not be easy for her to do this, because it is not so easy to bend most of your wills to suits someone else will. However, just because you want to attract this person in question to yourself, then being willing to conform to his will would not be a big deal.

Chapter 5

8. Holds Similar Values as you do

As a woman, men want you to have many similar values with them. In a way that would make both of you love the same things and dislike the same things. Just like the rest of my other points of things men look out for in a woman, and not a lot of women know about this mystery. As a woman you should not just live your life anyhow, you should not only think that things happen in life by chance, what life gives to use, if what we offer to it.

You cannot plant corn and expect to harvest cassava. So, therefore, whatever the case may be, what you give is what you get back in return. If you give love it is expected that you should be given love again in return also if you have similar values with someone you are feeling as though you are falling in love with, then you would realize that it would in a way result in a more natural communication with your partner.

Now, the things that we value all depend on our family background or in other words the way we are raised as children. As we are being raised as children, many things were bestowed on us in other to ensure that we are able to value some things more than others are. This value system from our childhood is what is affecting us in this present time.

These we find important are the things that affect our sense of value when we are much older. Now, many men out there probably had the best childhood and would probably want to go back to that time when all they did was just eat, sleep, play and repeat the cycle. Not like now when all they do is work, and work again with little rest, stressed out and worn out. Men would actually give anything just to go back to that moment. Therefore, as a woman who can share the same values with a man, you are indirectly helping him relive his childhood memories.

It is not that impossible to have similar values with a man you love. It may not be the same values word for word, but they would still feature the same meanings. Also, if at all, you do not really have the same values, and you feel like the love you have for this man supersedes any of it, then you can really consider working on getting some of the benefits that you have noticed to be present in the man. For example, if you see that he has a very high value for sports, and you are not a sports person, you can still try to understand what the games he loves so much are all about.

Developing values may be a bit stressful especially if the value is something you have never heard of then you may run into a few problems developing them. However, one thing is sure, and that is nothing is impossible if you put your mind into it. Therefore, do not feel overwhelmed when you are trying to develop similar values with someone you care about, and it just seems like you may never get there. You just need to be patient and persevere, and the sky would be your starting point.

9. Physically attractiveness

Well, this is quite an obvious one, but men would not say it to your face that they need you as a woman to be attractive. Actually, if they need to tell you, by all means, they would suggestively know you. Perhaps, both of you are out maybe shopping, or on a date and an attractive woman walks past both of you, he would comment on the women look and ask for your opinion. This way, making you try to see the reasons why you need to be like the woman, but he would not say it to your face that he wants you to be attractive.

Moreover, when you are attractive as a woman, it helps boost your self-esteem. You tend to feel a lot more confident in yourself. You can walk past anywhere and not feel intimidated because you know that in the corner of everyone's mind they know that you are attractive and they by all means either want to talk to you.

Being physically attractive is not really all about your skin complexion, or the shape of your nose, or how big your boobs are. Although I must confess they do add to how physically attractive a woman can look, but the bottom line is that as a woman to be physically attractive means how you can make yourself look good with what you have. A well-packaged product demands a higher price, so also with that same mentality package you correctly, dress appropriately, make your hair look beautiful, look enticing and appealing.

You do not necessarily need to go to the extreme, after all, you cannot wear make all day and all night in your own home, so try not to go too strict when it comes to wearing makeup in other to look attractive. Because if you do, you tend to create this kind of image in your lover's mind, and if eventually you both get married. Then there may be a little problem because your husband would start feeling as though you are getting ugly when you start cutting down on your make up.

Moreover, the main reason why men love it when women look attractive is that when they are with you as a beautiful woman, they would be more proud of themselves and of you also as they would have a feeling that they have gotten a significant achievement. They tend always to want to take you out, to flaunt you to the whole world. Also, to top it all, you would be like a priceless gem in his eyes.

Chapter 6

10.   Friendly and Sociable

Now the last quality on my list is in two folds, and that is as a woman you need to be friendly and sociable. Men generally have a great time hanging out with a friend more than anything does, this is because a friend to them is someone that knows just how they feel even when they have not said a single world. A friend to them is someone that knows how to cheer them up when they are feeling low, someone they go for advice and a confidant they can tell anything to.

Moreover, to be friendly as a woman means you have to be sociable. Being sociable these days is not really a big deal since we are in the era of social media, but one thing remains constant, when you are sociable, you would be attractive to men. Being friendly is not meant to be a big deal to do, as it only requires you to be kind and when you are kind then you would realize that being friendly just comes out of you naturally.

Being friendly can be a bit challenging most especially when you are trying to be friendly to a man that is rude. For you to be able to use your friendly nature to attract a man then you need to understand that the person you are trying to be as friendly as you can has to be friendly too, or at least try to be friendly. When someone is not friendly to you when you are trying to be friendly to the person is just a big spoiler. It may just seem like a perfect waste of time. You tend to feel a lot more discouraged in even trying to be noticed by the person.

Men love to be with a friendly woman because they are more caring and understanding. In addition, they can count on them. When you are also friendly as a woman, it would be a whole lot easier to communicate with you. Men love it when they can easily approach their lover and talk to them without feeling rejected or neglected. In addition, there is that sense of appreciation also. To attract that man to yourself as a woman, or to win him over also, then you need to consider being a friendly person. In addition, you need to consider being sociably, free to interact with him.

Having said all this 10 different character that every woman needs to know in other to be able to win a man's heart, I hope you were able to understand this things and how important they are. When you check yourself out and you notice that you do not really have a lot of these characters men look out for I a woman, then you should consider working on yourself in other to build up a couple of them.

If you can try to ensure you have all 10 of the characters, because men differ from each other, and to some men, they take some of these characters a little more serious than other. They place a kind of compulsoriness on some than they do on others. So, check yourself out, based on the things you do and the things you love to do, and know for sure who you really are, and I the end you will be able to win that man you what to attract or better still just be a very desirable person as a whole.

Conclusion

Thank you again for downloading this book!

I hope this book was able to help you to help you understand the different things men look out for in a woman. As a woman, you need to understand that you need to posses some certain characters. These characters are what men look out for but they do not want you to know, in fact, they would look out for it in a way that you would not even realize that they are really in search for some certain things.

The next step is to is to check your self, examine yourself to know the different characters that you have. After doing that have a checklist and make the ones you feel are the good ones, then try to crosscheck it with the ones I have given in this book. If you realize that at the end you do not really have sufficient character in your checklist then you may need to work on yourself to develop them.

Finally, if you enjoyed this book, then I'd like to ask you for a favor, would you be kind enough to leave a review for this book on Amazon? It'd be greatly appreciated!

Thank you and good luck!